ARE YOU

IN

or

OUT

VESTA RACHAEL GAUNTLETT

ARE YOU IN OR OUT?

First published in 2026 by Onyx Publishing, an imprint of Notebook Group Limited, London (W1W 5PF) Office, 167-169 Great Portland Street, 5th Floor, London, W1W 5PF.

www.onyxpublishing.com
ISBN: 9781913206796

A CIP catalogue record for this book is available from the British Library.

Typeset by Onyx Publishing of Notebook Group Limited.

For Delaney, Kalleigh, Michelle, Reagan and Elle
Thank You for believing in me, supporting my dream
and for reminding me that the best journeys are never
taken alone.

To every couple standing at a crossroads.

To the ones asking hard questions.

To the ones tired of pretending.

To the ones asking if a future is still possible.

May this book remind you that the next chapter

is not written by circumstance but by choice.

TABLE OF CONTENTS

v

AUTHOR'S NOTE

I believe a marriage based on mutual love, respect, and goals is worth all the work that goes into it.

This book is a gift. If it was given to you, that means whoever bought it for you still cares enough about the relationship to want to try and reconnect with you, to be excited about a future with you and to make the time and effort to heal and grow with you.

The question is, do you still care enough?

HOW TO READ THIS BOOK

ix

Guidelines:

1. Be honest (this includes being honest with yourself, too). This will save you both time. Life is short!
2. Complete this book in one sitting. It was purposefully designed to be read in a quick and concise manner.
3. Trust the process.
4. Print the worksheet, found at www.vestatalks.com and fill out as directed.
5. You create your own future. You choose, right here and right now. Lead with your heart.

Let the adventure begin!

TO BE CLEAR

x

This book is a gift. If you have it, that means your spouse:

- Still sees a life with you.
- Still cares enough to try.
- Still cares enough!

Do *you* still care enough? Let's find out.

If you bought this book for yourself, it is still a gift.

To find the path forward that will fulfill your needs is to put yourself first. This is not easy to do, and I applaud you for starting that journey.

xi

HUSBAND

SPOUSE

PARTNER

xii

Every Man has two opportunities in life, either stand up and be the man she needs you to be or sit down so she can see who's next in line.

~T. G.

TO A HUSBAND:

AN INTRODUCTION

Why did I write this book? Who am I?

First, I will tell you who I am not.

I am not a therapist, counselor, or psychiatrist. So, why did I write a book for married couples who aren't living the life that they expected to be? Simply, because I've been in your wife's (spouse's/partner's) shoes; I've felt what she's feeling. In my first marriage, I had the conversation so many times in my head, yet it took me years to actually say the words. Years wasted, because I didn't know how to get to my point across in a way that would make him hear my words— really *hear* them. I had to be stronger than I realized, to be direct, stop giving hints, and stop bringing it up then letting it go. I had to make sure he knew that this time, I was serious.

If your wife has ever said anything about wanting to work on your marriage, then I can guarantee she has thought about it a thousand times, probably for years. This book in your hands is proof that the time has come to have the conversation, properly.

Where should you start? Right here. This book is a great tool to help start a dialogue, because it will help you share common vocabulary and have a productive conversation about your future. It will create structure and offer support around this conversation. Above all, this book empowers you to choose your path forward. You literally hold your future in your hands.

I will share a few guidelines for this adventure.

- Be honest. Don't lie, even to yourself.
- Choose with an open heart the path that you truly feel you should follow.
- Be ready to accept either path with grace, respect, and joy.

This is the most important conversation you will ever have. I hope you give it the consideration you both deserve.

XOXO,
Vesta

CHOOSE WHAT FEELS RIGHT

Your heart already knows the answers to all your questions. Listen to it and choose the option that feels right.

- This is stupid. We don't need this book. It's a waste of time and money. We're just fine. Go to Page 43 "You Are Really Not Getting It."

- I know our life isn't perfect, but I didn't realize it was this bad. I want to work it out. Go to Page 19, "Breaking Old Patterns."

- So, we fight. We've been here before: something triggers a fight—a fight we've had a hundred times—but then things die down and go back to normal. This time is no different. Go to Page 53, "Ending Those Fights."

2

The strongest couples are not the ones who never break, they are the ones who learn to mend.

~Elle Lundy

GOOD CHOICE

You've made your choice, now what?

Let's talk about triggers and fights.

On your worksheet (which can be printed at www.vestatalks.com), there are some areas to complete. The goal is to have talking points, not fighting words; to de-escalate the conversation and gain positive traction. This will give you your best shot of being heard.

For example, let's say you forgot to take out the trash. This leads to your wife complaining as soon as you get home. She reminds you that you forgot again, that you hardly help around the house, and she has to do everything.

The fight commences.

Resolution:

In the future, take out the trash before she asks you to. It really is that simple. Yes, you sometimes forget, are running late, or don't want to, but whenever you remember to, do it anyway, *before she has a chance to ask*. She is probably tired, too, and this shows her you care for and respect her. Over time, she will be so pleasantly surprised by your initiative that you will slowly rebuild your trust, intimacy, and teamwork.

Remember, you are on the same team, you live in the same house, and you are going in the same direction toward the same future.

 On your worksheet, list at least three triggers that often lead to fights. If you need more space, print additional worksheets.

To continue to break negative patterns, go to Page 35, "Continuing the Work."

6

If you refuse to set a bold goal for your financial future, you're really setting a goal anyway: to keep things the way they are.

~Randy Gage

SOME FINANCIAL ADVICE*

Since many fights are about money and how we spend it, I suggest getting on the same page and working together. This will build trust and respect.

- Create shared goals for investing, saving, and future planning. If you have kids, also discuss 529s or college funds and custodial IRAs.

- Share responsibility of money. Working as a team means sharing control of finances. No one should be made to feel that they are being controlled or are on an allowance. This can create unhealthy power dynamics, animosity, and future debt issues.

- Have a shared bank account. Sharing an account means sharing accountability.

To continue to break negative patterns, go to Page 35, "Continuing the Work."

*I am not accountant, financial planner, or fiduciary. This is from personal experience.

YOU MISS HER

You want to feel closer and build intimacy, but how do you do that?

Send her flowers. Reward her with a spa day. Leave a note on her dashboard telling her she's beautiful,  smart, amazing, and incredible. Out of the blue, send her the video of your first dance from your wedding. Leave a menu from your first date where she will find it. Be creative. You know her best, and you know what will make her feel special. How did you get her to marry you in the first place? You made her feel seen, loved, cherished, and special. You still have the ability to do that. If you want more time with her, you need to make her feel that way again.

On your worksheet, write a list of things you can do to make her feel special. (Yes, I mean right now! Take a few minutes to physically write them down.) When she feels seen and appreciated, she will then be open to trusting you again. The hope here is to build intimacy.

This process will take time. Don't just pick one thing you know she loves and then be mad when she doesn't respond with love and trust immediately. You are rebuilding something that took years to create. Be patient and persistent. Show her you mean it. Set reminders on your phone. Commit to her happiness. Be creative and don't stop showing her you mean it and that you think she is worth it.

Guidance for working on this further can be found on Page 57, "Ideas to Make Her Feel Seen and Appreciated."

THE DANGERS OF ALWAYS HAVING TO BE "RIGHT"

Let's say you are getting into the car to go somewhere. Your spouse starts to enter the address in the GPS, but you already know how to get there.

You either:

- Say something, you tell them not to put the GPS on because you know the way. Then you have the fight, which ends in them keeping the GPS on. You fume all the way there, thinking that they don't trust or value you. When you arrive, you are both upset and feel disrespected. Go to Page 27, "Lost with No Direction."

OR (hint hint)

- Say nothing, so that you both arrive in a good mood and feel respected. Go to Page 55, "Ahh... Hear That?".

Remember, with either choice, you end up at the same place.

12

When you must choose between being kind and being right, choose kindness and you'll always be right.

~Michelle Victoria

MONEY, MONEY, MONEY

Let me guess: when you start talking about it, when you try saving it, or when you are spending it, you have a fight. It's like someone rings a bell and the round begins.

If your "main fight" is around finances, that isn't a surprise. Financial stress is a top marital concern.

There are many theories on the best way to manage money as a couple. You will find books on the *Resource Page* that I recommend you read together to help establish healthy financial planning.

The goal is to break patterns and diffuse triggers. Once you are on the same page about money, you can start to work toward shared goals. That is a W.I.N.

On the *Resource Page*, check out the Marriage Adventure Information for a W.I.N. (What is Next) event, during which you can plan your exciting future together. No matter where you are in the process of working toward your future goals, W.I.N. will take money talks from where they are today to where you want them to be. Focusing on shared future goals for tomorrow makes for a stronger today.

Go to Page 7, "Some Financial Advice."

WHAT MAKES YOU FEEL LOVED

You know you'd rather choose "less than perfect" with her over anything with someone else. Let's face it: life isn't perfect, if I am bursting your bubble, I am sorry. Still, we can foster a connection and life that is great if we can define what makes us feel loved and joyful.

Select the options that feel right to you.

- Intimacy (hugs, kisses, and real conversations). We are referring to connecting on a level like when you were first dating. Do you remember when you would do anything for even just a few minutes with her? Go to Page 9, "You Miss Her"

- Time. Just time. It's that simple. No distractions, no kids, doing something or nothing, just the two of you. Go to Page 45, "Finding the Time for Quality Time."

- More time with friends without being made to feel guilty or her being upset. Go to Page 23, "Time with Friends"

If there is something else you think would make things better, get out your worksheet and jot it down so it isn't overlooked. How can you show her you appreciate her and all that she does for you?

Stop acting as if life is a rehearsal. Live this day as if it were your last. The past is over and gone. The future is not guaranteed.
~Wayne Dyer

BREAKING OLD PATTERNS

Breaking patterns is hard, but so is making new ones. Sometimes, it's even harder.

Rehashing old patterns makes everyone in the equation feel bad. It does not serve your ultimate goal of a happier relationship. So, let's recognize them and choose to respond differently.

If you haven't filled in your worksheet on Triggers/Fights/Resolutions, do so now. If you can't think of any, I call bullshit on that. You know there is something your spouse does that drives you crazy for no real reason at all. Write it down.

For Instance, your spouse *always* turns the GPS on when you're the one who's driving, even though you've been to your destination twenty times. In this situation, you can:

- Tell them (for the 21st time) that you know the way and don't need the annoying GPS lady. Go to Page 27, "Lost with No Direction"

    OR (hint, hint!)

- Accept that *they* need it, and that this does not reflect their view of your navigation skills. Go to Page 55, "Ahh... Hear That?"

20

You must understand that the touch of your hand
makes my pulse react.
~As sung by Tina Turner

CREATING YOUR NEW FUTURE

Your first step to a more fulfilled marriage has been taken. You know about the value of bringing joy (Joy Jar forever!), you know and have memorized your new mantra (not my circus, not my monkeys), and you've cleared the way for a teamwork approach to finances, communication, respect, and love. You have been busy, and you are ready to shine.

Congratulations! This is the time when the work you put in reaps a direct result.

- Cherish your newfound commitment.

- Revisit this book when needed. Keep it on a bookshelf where you can easily grab it if things are getting tough again. Just seeing the book might inspire your spouse (or you) to get things back on track!

- Love one another the way you each need to be loved.

For further connection opportunities, you can locate extra exercises like the Ideal Day and Values and Goals on our website. www.vestatalks.com.

Sign up for a W.I.N. Event and be in love! All events can be located at www.vestatalks.com/events

Time with Friends is important as long as it's in addition to time spent with her, not as a replacement of Quality Time.

~Vesta

TIME WITH FRIENDS

Okay, so you like hanging out with the guys. We get that. We really do. Sometimes, we want time alone or time with our friends, too. This usually becomes a problem, however, when you are doing it *every* weekend, and every hangout starts early and ends late, you start skipping out on things that you would usually do together, such as kids' activities, church, and family meals.

If she feels like she is doing it all on her own, then she will think that she might as well do it all on her own "for real." In other words, you are slowly losing your footing in the relationship.

If she is left to manage every busy weekend and most evenings alone while you are off with the guys, this will not end well for you, resentment will build. Eventually, she will realize she can do it all without you, because she's already doing it. This is especially true if she values quality time as a way of feeling loved and connected.

I am sure some alarm bells are going off in your head as you're reading this, so listen up.

Whenever this becomes an issue, you may think, "I just want to hang out with my friends. Why does she care what I am doing?" To this I say, it likely isn't the specific thing that you are doing that is grating on her; it is the fact that you are rarely (or never) choosing to spend that time with her.

I get it; you need guy time. Again, this usually only becomes an issue when you see your guy friends *instead* of being with her and the family, not *in addition* to that.

Put this on your worksheet. One solution could be, you discuss it with her and pick a weekend or two that you will spend with your friends, and the rest will be dedicated to a balance of family time, fun time, together time, and "me" time. By having the discussion and scheduling it, she will feel less resentful, and you will be more present for important moments. Being there to see the winning goal or the dance recital matters; kids notice when you aren't there, and they will tell you about it years later. Be present in all your relationships.

You are a team, and you both need to recharge. The huge bonus is you will enjoy your time with your friends more when you know your spouse isn't sitting at home fuming at you. Plus, your kids will feel secure in the knowledge that you'll always be there when it counts.

Let's add even more joy. Head on over to Page 31, "The Joy Jar."

26

Don't let your ego destroy your relationship.

~Vesta

LOST WITH NO DIRECTION

27

So, you couldn't help yourself: you told them again, didn't you?

I know change is hard, but your need to be right does not enhance your intimacy and connection. The more you choose intimacy over being right, the closer you will become as a couple. This will foster love and respect.

To get what you really want in your relationship, Go to Page 11, "The Dangers of Always Having to be Right" and choose the answer that brings you closer together. Remember, the goal is for both of you to feel loved, respected, and *happy*!

Pick your battles. You don't have to show up to every
argument you're invited to.

~ Mandy Hale.

THE "MY WAY OR THE HIGHWAY" WIFE

I know you are familiar with this personality type if you made it to this page.

If you want more time with your spouse but you know that you "helping" with the chores will not go over well, find another solution. There are always specific things that help a person to feel more loved (remember the Joy Jar doesn't have to make sense).

Speak to her about how you have noticed she is very busy (you will get points right away just for that simple observation), tell her you miss her (as in, having undivided attention, just the two of you), and say that you want to help.

You will have to stow your own ego and do things her way if she accepts your offer. Maybe how the laundry is folded is super important to your spouse and not doing it her way is not helping. It just means (from her perspective) that she will have to do it over which will irritate her further.

 Say your wife loads the dishwasher a certain way, and you are sure your way is more efficient, i.e. right. If you truly are trying to help her, load the dishwasher her way. You will have to bite your tongue, but it will help you foster connection with your spouse. And the dishes will still be clean.

I know you have your own ideas about how the things in her Joy Jar should be done. This is not the time or place to share them. She is not interested in how you think T-shirts should be folded (even if you sincerely think your method is better). No matter what you are thinking about her approach, she does not want to hear it; she just wants you to play ball.

Remember, your goal is for her to spend more time with you *and* not be angry at you. So, learn to clean the bathroom, fold towels, or whatever she agrees to let you help with, *her* way. Smile and learn. Just keep smiling and you will build intimacy and trust.

There is going to be a lot of trial and error, so stay humble, and it will pay off. If you need to vent, use the voice app on your phone and tell her how your way is better.

Then, delete it. No really, delete it. And keep raising her joy.

Go to Page 37, "Intimacy and Connection."

THE JOY JAR
ALLOW ME TO SET THE SCENE:

She's having a great morning. The coffee is aromatic. She gazes out the window and smiles at the sunshine. Then, she sees the dishes in the sink, on the "wrong" side (according to her monkey), and she loses her shit (and a bit of her joy).

It goes on like that throughout the day.

It's simple math: you want to keep her joy *up* ↑ and her irritation *down* ↓.

The goal of the Joy Jar is to share these little grievances with one another without confrontation or denial. There is no need for a discussion about them, because there is nothing to discuss. Maybe they can tell you why having the shoes lined up at the door properly really matters to them, or maybe they can't. It doesn't matter why; not really. They probably can't explain their quirk—their monkey—but the Joy Jar offers a safe space for them to share those details and make your lives better.

It is simple: you take a jar and two different slips of colored paper. You fill out what matters to you, and you agree to do or not do those things without discussion. You agree to bring more joy to the relationship. Your spouse is telling you *exactly* what will bring more joy to your life and relationship. Why wouldn't you want to know that?

Here is the solution: stop doing "the thing," or start doing "the thing," whichever fixes this monkey. Most of the time, "the thing" isn't really a big deal in theory, but it is to your spouse.

By honoring their requests, you are being respectful. This will increase mutual joy.

The key rules here are simple:

1. As your monkeys rear their little heads (this means something that your spouse has done bothers you; it is not a big thing, but it drives you crazy), use the colored paper assigned to you and write it down. Remember, "the thing" doesn't have to "make sense." (Why does it matter that they put the toilet paper roll on the holder the wrong way? It just does.)

2. You must select at least one of your spouse's papers a week and commit to doing that for her. Even if it makes no sense to you why it would matter, remember, they are her monkeys. She doesn't need to explain or justify; she simply needs to know that you are willing to hear her out. By making these little changes, you are adding joy to her day and your marriage. That is a win-win in the easiest of terms. (Feel free to do more than one if you are eager to increase her joy—which you should be!)

3. Even though we know what to do (or what they want us to do), sometimes we can't bring ourselves to do it. I have seen this unfold in my own relationships.

If there is something she has requested that you can't or won't do, you need to have a discussion about it. Make time for this conversation. The problem won't go away by ignoring it.

The goal here is that eventually, the jar will be empty nearly all the time (a few notes may get put in when we slip up).

An entirely empty jar means you are both more joyful, and that is good news for you.

 Why? Well, let's say you have kept her joy level high, and she is coasting by on a cloud of love and appreciation. One day, you let her know while on your way to work that you want to head out for a drink with the guys that evening. In this joyful state, she is all about making you happy, too, so she responds, "Have a great time." The joy has multiplied.

Alternatively, let's just say you are rarely home, you hardly help out, and you continue to do all the things that are filling up the Joy Jar. Then, you ask about that drink out. Her response will not be full of joy: "Sure, go.

Leave me here to handle everything. Have a great time."

Obviously, this is extreme marital sarcasm. She *doesn't* want you to have a good time. She may barely care if you make it back.

No joy = not good for you or your marriage.

When joy levels are low, spouses know. My spouse could read my vibe. He knew that there was an issue when as he was heading out for the day, I could only manage a, "Don't die," as we said goodbye. Clearly, he'd messed with my joy when I've reached this low point. My advice? Avoid this scenario.

For more information, turn to the Resource page.

If you haven't been to Page 47, "The Monkeys: Building Intimacy and Trust" yet, please read now.

CONTINUING THE WORK

35

Let's keep breaking old patterns and rediscovering that spark.

- If you want to improve all aspects involved in a fulfilled marriage. Go to Page 55, "Ahh... Hear That?"

- If you want to stop hurting each other with your old destructive patterns. Go to Page 19, "Breaking Old Patterns."

- If your "main fight" is about money. Go to Page 13, "Money, Money, Money."

- If you need to define how you feel love. Go to Page 15. "What makes you feel loved"

A woman becomes a reflection of how you treat her.
If you don't like how she acting, take a good look at
yourself.

~Delaney Jensen

INTIMACY AND CONNECTION

So, you have carved out some time to spend together. You've also been helping around the house, and she has noticed. Now, how do you start to use that time together to build intimacy and connection?

For you, an ideal evening together may involve watching a movie on the couch. This, to you, would make you feel loved and connected. But this may not be aligned with *her* idea of intimacy. (And yes, what she wants matters too.)

In my experience, hardly anyone marries someone who feels loved the same way they do. This leads to some complicated relationships. It is possible for two people who feel love the same way to end up together, but in my very detailed (unscientific) research, I have found that probability points toward this not being your situation.

Maybe in the beginning, you both shared interests and pulled each other out of your comfort zones. Everything felt new and exciting, and you loved everything about them. But now, you feel far apart. You miss the intimacy and connection you had, and she probably misses it too.

To get back your spark, list three things you used to enjoy doing together and put them on your worksheet for Discussion Day.

Start thinking about plans you could make to reignite those connections. Be creative in the planning and in how you ask her on these dates.

Do not approach this like a normal date or a casual Wednesday night dinner. Making it special will make *her* feel special.

List three new things you would like to explore such as hiking, trivia nights, or escape rooms. Think of creative ways in which you can ask her to try these out with you. New experiences tap into that first-time feeling and build intimacy. Be open to the ideas on her list as well.

Maybe unwrap a new Trivial Pursuit game and organize a game night with friends or buy her a new pair of hiking boots. Everyone likes to feel appreciated, and showing that you put in the effort, organized the date and asked her out, makes her feel wooed again.

You alone have the power to make your spouse feel that she is the only woman for you every day (not just on the day you married). Do not be afraid to use this power to increase the joy in your marriage.

To define how you are loved, Go to Page 15, "What makes you feel loved."

If you know how you are loved Go to Page 41, "Moving Forward Together."

Marriage is not a revolving door; you're either in or you're out.

~Unknown

MOVING FORWARD TOGETHER

You are now aware of what you both need in the relationship. You are also taking steps to be more present and increase the joys of each day. Your persistence will pay off, trust me.

If you haven't been to Page 31, "The Joy Jar" or Page 47, "The Monkeys: Building Intimacy and Trust," please read those now. Be ready to implement their teachings and watch the relationship grow.

Review your worksheet and be ready to compare notes and work together toward an exciting future.

If you have already read "The Joy Jar" and "The Monkeys: Building Intimacy and Trust," please turn to Page 21 "Creating Your New Future."

42

Shot through the heart and you're to blame.

~ As sung by Bon Jovi

YOU ARE REALLY NOT GETTING IT

You were given this book because everything is *not* fine. Not at all. You may not want to face it, admit it, or try to fix it, but it is a fact.

The person who gave this to you thinks you are worth the cost of this book and that your life together is worth thirty minutes of your time. They still want to be with you but in a healthier, happier relationship.

Check your ego! Do *you* want to reconnect and create a marriage where you both feel respected and loved?

If your answer is no, turn to Page 59, "Moving On."

If you realize that you picked this option out of denial (FYI, you totally did), I get it; you're scared. But if you still love her, go back to Page 1, "Choose What Feels Right" and choose again. You are literally holding your life and future in your hands. It is up to you what you do with it.

If your answer is yes, go to Page 3, "Good Choice."

FINDING TIME FOR QUALITY TIME

You miss spending time with her, the girl you married; the woman you love; the person who, by giving you this book, still chooses you. You know she is busy, whether a mother, a career woman, or a CEO, she is a contributing partner. She may also have other responsibilities to maintain the home and child related responsibilities such as: driver, laundress, personal shopper, maid, childcare provider, chief boo-boo kisser, or the only one who can read a bedtime story (according to the kids).

But she is your wife too. She is the woman you chose, forsaking all others. And sometimes, we wives and mothers feel there isn't enough time and we want more of it.

To get more time with her... you have to *make* more time for her.

 For a few days, watch her and determine what things take up her time. Identify at least three things you could step in and help with. The dishes? Dinner? Grocery shopping? Vacuuming? Laundry? Ironing? School lunches? The kids' drop-offs, or homework, or projects? These are just some ideas, but if quality time is how you feel loved, she will need you to help her gain some of her time back first

Make a plan and start helping. No woman is ever going to be mad to find a clean kitchen, folded laundry, or finished homework. (If this backfires because she has control issues and she only wants it done her way, turn to Page 36, "The 'My Way or the Highway' Wife"). She probably won't know how to react at first, but be consistent. If you see it needs to be done, do it. As she starts to have more time, that is your chance to ask her to join you on the porch for a glass of wine or to sit by the firepit.
You are making time for her to *enjoy* time with you. This is a win-win that is full of joy for you both. And a happy mama means happier kids, too!

Go to Page 37, "Intimacy and Connection."

If you feel your wife may resist your *help*. Go to page 29, "The 'My Way or the Highway Wife'"

THE MONKEYS: BUILDING INTIMACY AND TRUST

One way to build intimacy is through *trust*. When you question your spouse's motives, habits, and choices, they feel you do not trust them. How do you nip this in the bud? Well, sometimes, something comes up that is just *not* your problem. Really. It is *not yours*. I have a phrase to remind me to exercise trust instead of judgment.

Not my circus, not my monkeys.

Say it out loud. Repeat it. Let it sink in. Seems silly, right? But this is a marriage lifesaver. Saying this instead of whatever you want to say (trust me, she does *not* want to hear whatever "advice" you were going to give) does two things:

1. It stops any argument cold in its tracks. Suddenly, there is nothing to argue about.

2. It shows your spouse that you trust her decisions (even if deep down inside, you think you are *right* and she is wrong).

 Maybe your spouse is about to make a smoothie. They've overfilled the container, *in your opinion*, and because you are always *right* and want to *help*, you

are about to open your mouth to tell them that they are screwing up and are going to make a big mess.

But wait: you remember that being over-judgmental isn't going to help. Instead, do nothing, look away if you have to, but do *not* give your *advice*.

Meanwhile, your spouse knows your "I told you so" is pending and is waiting for you to offer your "advice." They are prepared for you to throw the first "know it all" verbal punch. There is tension in the air.

What they don't know is that you have already remembered your new mantra: *Not my circus, not my monkeys.* This is their circus. You are just in the audience. Smile and go about your business. Nothing to see here, folks. It will be hard, but the good news is it will get easier, and it will bring more joy to you both.

Now, here's the hard part: if or when the smoothie overflows and makes a mess, *do not*:

1. Say "I told you so" or "I was going to tell you."
2. Laugh and point.

   ...Or anything else.

It's not your circus or your monkeys. If they make a mess, they will clean it up, and anything you say will start a fight. Practice not giving your opinion in these situations. This way, you will slowly rebuild that trust from all the times you *didn't* keep quiet.

If you have not yet read Page 31, "The Joy Jar," do so now. If you have, turn to Page 21, "Creating Your New Future."

Before you decide whether to stay or leave, ask yourself one question: Do I feel more like myself here or less?

~Elle Lundy

SO, NOW YOU KNOW

To paraphrase a line from an underrated Adam Sandler movie, *Spanglish*, it's okay to realize that you still love your spouse.

The actual tasks that will help you improve your marriage are simple. The hard part is setting your ego aside. It is especially hard to do so when you are tired in the morning or running behind all day. In this situation, it is easy to fall into disruptive patterns and disrespectful behavior.

It sucks when you realize you've done this, but it is so familiar. It is like a siren calling you to wreck your marriage on the rocks of discontent. But you can do this. You *want* to choose your marriage and your spouse. You just didn't realize that choosing them meant also choosing their joy every day.

Marriage is hard, but by reading this book, I know you have the most important ingredient: hope.

True magic happens in the small changes that are made every day. You will have bad days, but you also have good tools. If you are short, rude, or dismissive, apologize immediately. You won't let it build up if you are building trust. No matter how many setbacks or Joy Jar notes it takes, the good news is, you are moving forward together.

Go to Page 55, "Ahh... Hear That?"

52

There are no unlockable doors, there are no unwinnable wars.

~Ozzy Osbourne

ENDING THOSE FIGHTS

So, you fight. Often. About the same things. Maybe we need to look at those triggers.

If you have this book in your hands, your spouse is *asking* for this cycle to stop, *now*. She is done with fighting, and she may be getting close to being done, period.

Nervous yet? You should be. When a woman gets to this point, it's rarely because of something that happened last week, last month, or even last year; it's because of a long-term recurring pattern that she's at the end of her rope with.

What can you do? Well, reading this book is a good start. Be honest now. This is about moving forward, and the path you take for that depends on your choice:

1. Do you even want to do anything to fix this, or are you done? Think about this hard. She deserves that. If you don't want to work on it, go to Page 59, "Moving On."

2. I am guessing you want to move forward together, since you are reading this option. I think she'd love for you to acknowledge the situation *and* the fact that you want to make it better. But how? Go to Page 7, "Some Financial Advice."

54

Life is rough, you gotta be tough.

-Johnny Cash

AHH... HEAR THAT?

No fighting.

You've made the choice that serves your relationship best. You've chosen intimacy and trust over being right. I know it wasn't easy, but it will get easier. Like with any new habit, you've just got to practice. You are on the road to creating a stronger connection with your spouse.

The bonus of this is, you arrive at your destination, and you aren't fuming about being ignored or feeling undervalued. They also feel happy and respected, because you trusted them to get you there. (Consider that maybe they use the GPS so *they* know the way and can think of other things, like talking to you, *not* because they don't trust you.)

When these kinds of situations come up, use this mantra:

Not my circus, not my monkeys.

It's true. It isn't your issue or need; it's *theirs*. This will let you focus on your business without poking your nose into theirs.

Let's build on that and go to Page 47, "The Monkeys: Building Intimacy and Trust."

56

I love her and that's the beginning and the end of everything.

~F. Scott Fitzgerald

IDEAS TO MAKE HER FEEL SEEN AND APPRECIATED

So, you've set reminders on your phone or used the Resource page for other ideas.

- You text her a sweet message that you miss her.
- You text her that she is amazing.
- You text her that you are so lucky she chose you.
- You tell her she is beautiful, how good dinner was, and that you appreciate your laundry being washed and put away.

Set yourself a reminder to give her at least three compliments a day, and make sure some are paid in person. This is very important if she feels loved by being seen, as compliments validate that for her. They especially mean a lot from you, as compliments often aren't given enough in marriages. Women (and men) can feel invisible within their relationships if they need verbal appreciation, and it is not given.

It gets easier the more you do it. Practice builds a habit.

Remember to say great things about her even if she isn't around. She will hear about how well you speak of her from her friends and others, and that will mean even more to her. Be consistent. She will need to believe that this is a new behavior she can trust in. She needs to know that you value her.

Keep it up and you will get her attention, in a good way. Continue to page 51 "So now you know."

To survive the tide, love divides.

~As sung by Journey

MOVING ON

59

Well, I did ask you to be honest. If this is how you feel, let's save everyone some time and get right to it.

You have let your partner know you do not want to stay in this marriage. You have decided that you want an amicable, fair, drama-free divorce. That is the only respectful choice.

You are grateful for:

- The time you've had together.
- The life you've shared.
- The family you've created (if applicable).

Seek mediation to finalize your divorce. Do not be petty or vengeful here. Be fair. Be quick. Remind yourself why you loved them and show respect when you speak about them and to them. Be the best version of yourself as you move on. Your kids are watching (if you have them), and they will remember how you both conduct yourselves during this time.

This person was a chapter (or many chapters) in the story of your life. Honor that experience and may both of you find love and joy again.

XOXO,
Vesta

Sometimes the most romantic thing you can do is stay
and do the work.

~Elle Lundy

RESOURCE PAGE

Books

- The 5 Love Languages: The Secret to Love that Lasts by Gary Chapman (1990, Northfield Publishing)
- Smart Couples Finish Rich: 9 Steps to Creating a Rich Future for You and Your Partner by David Bach (2001, Broadway)
- Start Late, Finish Rich: A No-Fail Plan for Achieving Financial Freedom at Any Age by David Bach (2005, Doubleday Canada)
- The Finish Rich Workbook: Get Out of Debt, Put Your Dreams in Action and Achieve Financial Freedom by David Bach (2005, Doubleday Canada)

Apps

Love Nudge is connected to Chapman's *The 5 Love Languages*. Take the quiz and share your love language with your spouse. Stay connected to your spouse and show love the way *they* feel it. Set goals and nudge each other to build your healthy relationship.

*I am not affiliated with, nor am I compensated, by any of these resources.

Retreats and Adventures

The W.I.N. Marriage Adventure was created by Vesta Rachael Gauntlett.

This is more than a marriage retreat. It is an exclusive event featuring marriage workshops, unique experiences, and crafting an exciting plan for your future.

These retreats are held throughout the year, and their limited availability allows for dedicated couples to enjoy this experience, grow, and reconnect. See website for details, and to reserve your spot. www.vestatalks.com/events.

ABOUT THE AUTHOR

Vesta Gauntlett is an author, speaker, and retreat host who helps couples courageously ask the question many avoid: Are we In or Out?

She is the creator of the W.I.N. Marriage Adventure (What Is Next), an intimate luxury experience designed to help couples reconnect, rediscover their spark, and intentionally design an exciting future together.

Through her work, Vesta encourages couples to choose their relationship with clarity, courage, and a little adventure.

Vesta splits her time between the Pacific and Inland Northwest with her family, and is looking forward to her next adventure.

ARE YOU IN or OUT

VESTA RACHAEL GAUNTLETT

For Delaney, Kalleigh, Michelle, Reagan and Elle
Thank You for believing in me, supporting my
dream and for reminding me that the best journeys
are never taken alone.

On the cusp of the before heading into the after.

~ Elle Lundy

To every couple standing at a crossroads.
To the ones asking hard questions.
To the ones tired of pretending.
To the ones asking if a future is still possible.
May this book remind you that the next chapter
Is not written by circumstance but by choice.

HOW TO READ THIS BOOK

Guidelines:

1. Be honest (this includes being honest with yourself, too). This will save you both time. Life is short!
2. Complete this book in one sitting. It was purposefully designed to be read in a quick and concise manner.
3. Trust the process.
4. Print the worksheet, found at www.vestatalks.com and fill out as directed.
5. You create your own future. You choose, right here and right now. Lead with your heart.

Let the adventure begin!

TABLE OF CONTENTS

Before you decide whether to stay or leave, ask yourself one question: Do I feel more like myself here or less?

~Elle Lundy

WIFE
SPOUSE
PARTNER

Some relationships are worth a whole bottle, others
were only meant to be a single toast.

~Elle Lundy

TO A WIFE:

AN INTRODUCTION

Allow me to introduce myself.

I am a wife, a mother, a divorcee, and a hopeful romantic. I believe we all have a right to be happy and respected. I believe we all deserve love.

I wrote this book for couples who genuinely care for one another and who want more from their marriage: more love, more connection, more joy. It may also serve as a tool for those who need to move on but don't know how. The choices you make within this book will show the path forward.

Oftentimes, we find the hard conversations easier to avoid, or we get tired of pointing out issues and being ignored. I know I tried to start the conversation many times before I actually had it. I didn't want to hurt him or leave him lonely. But in the end, the conversation must happen, so you can either change and grow or move on. To delay it is only to prolong the hurt of the moment you are in.

Read the words on the pages of this book and choose your path with your heart. Be honest with yourself. No matter what path you end up choosing, you are strong enough to survive where it will take you.

Here, you will either commit to doing the work to strengthen your marriage, or you will develop the courage to respectfully move on.

The only way to find out what's next for you, is to be truthful and honest with yourself as you read this book.

You deserve a respectful and joyous marriage. You deserve to look to the future with hope. You deserve to be part of a hopeful partnership. You deserve to be cherished. You are worth so much more than you realize. I see you and you are magnificent. Be strong for yourself and your family. Your joy is waiting for you.

XOXO
Vesta

P.S. This book is a gift. If you have it, that means your spouse:

- Still sees a life with you.
- Still cares enough to try.
- Still cares enough!

Do *you* still care enough? Let's find out.

If you bought this book for yourself, it is still a gift.

To find the path forward that will fulfill your needs is to put yourself first. This is not easy to do, and I applaud you for starting that journey.

CHOOSE WHAT FEELS RIGHT

Your heart already knows the answers to all your questions, so choose the option that feels right.

- We keep having the same fights and disappointments. I am *not* happy; he is *not* happy. This is not the life I want for us as a family or a couple. Simply put, it is not the life I want. Go to Page 17, "Honesty is the Only Policy."

- We're fine. We don't fight. In fact, we don't talk. We are more like roommates. My heart feels like it is withering on the vine. Mutual neglect is killing us. Go to Page 21, "Alone Together is the Worst Kind of Lonely."

- We fight and we make up. Things between us are great—until they're not. Repeat *ad nauseum.* Go to Page 39, "If You Have to Ask..."

- Our main issue is money—what to do, to manage, save, and so on. Go to Page 11, "Money, Money, Money."

- I've known I wanted this for a while now, but it was easier to ignore it. I now can't any longer. Go to Page 3, "The Time Has Come."

Love should feel like a place you can exhale, not a place where you must hold your breath.

~Elle Lundy

THE TIME HAS COME

It sounds like you probably decided weeks, months, or maybe years ago that this was over. You stayed for your reasons, but you don't want to stay any longer.

If you have voiced your needs to him *and* you have made it clear (probably many times) that certain things are dealbreakers, then you have given him time to process. You have every right to expect the person who loves you to show you love in the way you *feel* love.

If it has become clear that he is not going to be that person for you, go to Page 57, "Moving On." He can still be a provider and father (if applicable) without you staying with him. How he shows up for his family is up to him.

It is time to create the loving life you want to be living *now*.

One of a parent's jobs is to show their kids what life can be. What kind of example does it set when all a child sees is disrespect and contempt between their parents?

~ K Jensen

Child of three divorces

SHOULD I STAY OR SHOULD I GO?

What is more unfair to the kids (if applicable): staying miserable and modeling that behavior, or choosing a healthy relationship?

Simply put, you want a fulfilling marriage, and you are not in one. That is how you feel every day. That is what you are *modeling* every day.

If there were resources, books, courses, and retreats that could help you in your marriage, would you be willing to explore them? Select your answer below.

- Yes, yes, yes, please. I want my marriage to be better than ever. If there is a way to make that happen, I want to try. Go to Page 55, "Is This What I Signed Up For?"

- I would, but I don't think he will do anything to work on it. I doubt he'll even read this book. Go to Page 13, "Will He Try?"

- We need help to break old patterns. Go to Page 7, "Breaking Old Patterns."

- It's hopeless. I'm tired of doing everything, being the only one who is concerned, and finding nothing that helps. I don't know if I can do it anymore. Go to Page 57, "Moving On."

BREAKING OLD PATTERNS

Breaking patterns is hard, but so is making new ones. Sometimes, it's even harder.

Rehashing old patterns makes everyone in the equation feel bad. It does not serve your goal. So, let's recognize them and choose to respond to them differently.

If you haven't filled in your worksheet on Triggers/Fights/Resolutions, do so now. If you can't think of any, I call bullshit on that. Fill it in as they occur to you. What is something your spouse does that drives you crazy for no real reason, but that still affects your relationship?

Maybe your spouse *always* turns the GPS on when you're the one who's driving, even though you've been to your destination twenty times. In this situation, you can:

- Tell them (for the 21st time) that you know the way and don't need the annoying GPS lady. Go to Page 35, "Lost with No Direction"

  or (hint, hint!),

- Accept that *they* need it, and that this does not reflect their view of your navigation skills. Go to Page 19, "Ahh… Hear That?"

QUALITY TIME

If you miss having time together, just the two of you, let him know. Put it on your worksheet and plan on ways to make time to spend together.

Maybe you will feel loved if you have his attention over a great meal. Book a date night and talk to each other, with no phones, no kids, and so on. Maybe think of a few topics beforehand to get the conversation flowing.

Maybe you like having new adventures or trying new things together. When you were first dating, were you always trying the newest fad, finding new trails to hike, or traveling? Rekindle those interests and get out and experience this amazing world together.

Maybe you used to always go see a movie on opening night, enjoying the anticipation and excitement of being one of the first ones to see it. Buy movie tickets and make it a date.

You need to be very clear about what it would look like for you to have more quality time in a way where you can build on your relationship together. Most men like knowing what it is that you want, and being clear lets them assimilate it into your life. Really think about how you feel the most loved and start to add those moments into your life.

Check the resource page for links to books and apps to help make it easier for you both to show love in the way your spouse feels it most.

To bring even more joy to your lives, go to Page 29, "The Joy Jar."

MONEY, MONEY, MONEY

Let me guess: when you start talking about it, when you try saving it, or when you try to stop spending it, you have a fight. It's like someone rings a bell and the round begins.

If your "main fight" is around finances, that isn't a surprise.

There are many theories on how is best to manage money as a couple. You will find books on the Resource page that I recommend you read together, to help establish healthy financial planning.

The goal is to break patterns and diffuse triggers. Once you are on the same page about money, you can start to work toward shared goals. That is a W.I.N.

Note: On the Resource page, check out our getaway W.I.N events. Start planning an exciting future together.

No matter where you are, working toward your future goals together will make you see that your money issues represent the distance between where you want to be in the future versus where you are today. Bringing focus to shared future goals today builds a stronger tomorrow. Go to Page 51, "Funding Your Future."

Either he will or he won't. Either way, you have your answer.

~Vesta

WILL HE TRY?

You are nervous and wonder if he will even read this book. You feel alone.

If he agrees to read it, then you've both acknowledged that you want to work on your marriage. That is the crucial first step.

This book aims to get partners on the same page and to choose a future right for them, whether it is apart or together. Whatever you choose, your new path will help you to create a new life with new possibilities. Be excited about that.

You can now choose the next steps together. Go to Page 35, "Lost with No Direction."

If he won't read the book, or you bought this for yourself to confirm what you've been feeling, you have your answer, and you can start your next chapter of life, even if that doesn't include him as your spouse. You can do this. Go to Page 57, "Moving On."

Passion is not a luxury in love; in some relationships
it is oxygen.

~Elle Lundy

AS OLIVIA SANG, "LET'S GET PHYSICAL!"

Connecting and building intimacy through touch is something I have a lot to say about. If you crave physical intimacy, tune in.

The act of touch of contact is a *choice*, *every time* it happens. This also means *not touching* is a choice, every time.

Let's say you feel loved through giving touch, but your spouse is phoning it in. Perhaps they give you a quick hug or a peck, which is *almost* what you want, by the simplest definition of touch, but you know they do this so that you can't say they didn't hug or kiss you. This becomes a mockery of what you need (which is almost worse than no touch at all). When they choose to *not* touch the way you need, it says, "I know you want hugs, kisses, and caresses, but I will only do it on my terms, just so you can't say it never happens. That means it still counts as a kiss even if I make monkey noises, lick your face, or slap your butt. A kiss is a kiss, so there." This is petty, and it hurts us even more. It matters to us to be cherished through touch, and when they make a face or a silly noise, they ensure it's distracting, disappointing, and not intimate at all.

What do you do in this situation?

Go to Page 23, "Reactions Tell a Tale."

The best relationships feel like partnerships, two people building a life neither could build alone.

~Elle Lundy

HONESTY IS THE ONLY POLICY

First, I want to congratulate you on being honest with yourself.

If he gave you this book, this is good news. He is telling you he doesn't want this life *as it is right now* either. He acknowledges that you aren't alone in wanting something different. He is also telling you he still wants to be with you.

Do *you* want to re-engage, re-connect, and re-imagine your life together? Go to Page 25, "Create Your New Future."

If you feel that you truly do not want to reconnect and have already moved on, this might be the right choice for you. Being honest is the only way to live the life you want to live. Go get your life. Go to Page 57, "Moving On."

Being invisible in your relationship is like standing in a crowded room, screaming at the top of your lungs, and no one is even glancing your way.

~ Michelle Victoria

AHH... HEAR THAT?

No fighting.

You've made the choice that serves your relationship best. You've chosen intimacy and trust over being right. I know it wasn't easy, but it will get easier. Like with any new habit, you've just got to practice. You are on the road to creating a stronger connection with your spouse.

The bonus is, you arrive at your destination, and you aren't fuming about being ignored or feeling undervalued. They also feel happy and respected, because you trusted them to get you there. (Consider that maybe they use the GPS so *they* know the way and can think of other things, like talking to you, *not* because they don't trust you.)

When these kinds of situations come up, use this mantra:

Not my circus, not my monkeys.

It's true. It isn't your issue or need; it's *theirs*. This will let you focus on your business without poking your nose into theirs.

Let's build on that and go to Page 45, "The Monkeys: Building Intimacy and Trust."

You can't wake a person who is pretending to be asleep.

~Navajo Proverb

ALONE TOGETHER IS THE WORST KIND OF LONELY

Neglect. Loneliness. These are our constant reminders that this is not what love is supposed to feel like.

I know some of my loneliest moments ever have been while sitting together on a couch just a few cushions apart. There is a tremendous difference between being alone and being lonely. But I don't need to tell you that. The solution is obvious, but just out of reach. It's *right there*. You can literally reach out and touch him. But you don't, because:

1. If you do, he will pull away, pat your hand, or put it on the cushion so you're not touching him; or, worse, he will tell you you're being clingy or interrupting his show. (Who would keep trying if they kept getting rejected?) So, you sit there dying inside and wishing it was different; that *he* was different. Go to Page 41, "Physical Touch."
2. If you ignore your needs for attention or touch and don't reach out, he'll think everything is fine and nothing will change. But something *must* change. Go to Page 33, "Intimacy."
3. You don't want to touch him anymore. You don't want to sit here quietly when inside, you are screaming for anything to change— even if that means big changes. Go to Page 1, "Choose What Feels Right."

REACTIONS TELL A TALE

This is hard, because if you've been married for any length of time, these aren't just discussions; they are relationship *bombs*.

You know you will get one of these reactions when you bring up this type of topic:

1. "Okay." (But nothing changes.)

2. "I already go out of my way to give you a kiss and a hug. It's not my love language, and I won't learn it."

3. "I have been trying, but I hear it hasn't been enough. What else can I do to make sure you feel loved? I really love you and our life together."

Most of us are very familiar with (1) and (2). Almost never do we get (3). But if we *don't* have that conversation, it will never change. And if they think we will let it go again (because we're frustrated, not because it doesn't matter), we will stay hurt and feel even more disconnected and unloved.

Put this on your Discussion Worksheet. Refer to the Resource Page for more information.

It's important that both partners feel *loved* in their language. They can't expect you to stay if they refuse to learn it. Period.

If he *will* discuss it, put it on your worksheet. If he won't, then you have his answer.

Go to Page 33, "Intimacy."

CREATE YOUR NEW FUTURE

The fact you are here tells me you are one hundred percent *in* and ready. Let your spouse know this, and pledge to restart your relationship with new respect, intimacy, and true commitment.

How do you get there?

- Retreats (for you and as a couple). My marriage adventures are designed just for you.

- The Resource page. This has a list of books and links for you to look over.

- Couples' counseling. This is a great option for many couples.

- A vow renewal.

- W.I.N. (What is Next) event. These are amazing experiences where you actually design your future together.

As a bonus activity, read pages "Create Your New Future" and "Intimacy" (Page 33) together!

Celebrate and mark this date. Go out to a fancy dinner, get dressed up, don't talk about the kids, and beam with the joy of love rekindled. You've earned this.

With all my love,

XOXO
Vesta

INCREASING JOY

It may be true that no one is blissfully happy all the time, but you can still improve your relationship in such a way where you make the happy times more frequent occurrences.

If you are both willing to build on happiness, you can find more joy. Go to Page 29, "The Joy Jar."

Joy is the most magnetic force in the universe.

~ Danielle LaPorte

THE JOY JAR:

ALLOW ME TO SET THE SCENE:

He's having a great morning. The coffee is aromatic. He gazes out the window and smiles at the sunshine. Then, he sees the dishes in the sink, on the "wrong" side (according to his monkey), and he loses his shit (and a bit of his joy).

It goes on like that throughout the day.

It's simple math: you want to keep his joy *up* ↑ and his irritation *down* ↓.

The goal of the Joy Jar is to share these little grievances with one another without confrontation or denial. There is no need for a discussion, because there is nothing to discuss. Maybe they can tell you why having the shoes lined up at the door properly really matters to them, or maybe they can't. It doesn't matter why; not really. They probably can't explain their quirk—their monkey—but the Joy Jar offers a safe space for them to share those details and make your lives better.

It is simple: you take a jar and two different slips of colored paper. You fill out what matters to you, and you agree to try and to bring more joy to the relationship. Your spouse is telling you *exactly* what will bring more joy to your life and relationship. Why wouldn't you want to know that?

Sometimes, even though we know what to do (or what they want us to do), we just can't bring ourselves to do it. Our ego is determined to make our spouse suffer, even if that means we suffer, too. (I am not a psychologist, but I have seen this unfold in my own relationships.)

There is a solution to this: stop doing "the thing," or start doing "the thing" (whichever fixes this monkey). Most of the time, "the thing" isn't really a big deal in theory, but it is to your spouse. By honoring their requests, you are being respectful. That will increase their joy *and* your joy.

The key rules here are simple:

1. As your monkeys rear their little heads (this means something that your spouse has done bothers you; it is not a big thing, but it drives you crazy), use the colored paper assigned to you and write it down. Remember, "the thing" doesn't have to "make sense." (Why does it matter that they put the toilet paper roll on the holder the wrong way? It just does.)

2. You must select at least one of your spouse's papers a week and commit to doing that for him. Even if it makes no sense to you why it would matter, remember, they are his monkeys. He doesn't need to explain or justify; he just needs to know that you are willing to hear him out. By making these little changes, you are adding joy to his day and your marriage. That is a win-win in the easiest of terms. (Feel free to do more than one if you are eager to increase his joy—which you should be!)

3. If there is something you have requested that you simply can't or won't do, then you need to have a discussion about it. Make time for this conversation. The problem won't go away by you ignoring it.

The goal here is that eventually, the jar will stand mostly empty all the time (a few notes may get put in when we slip up). An entirely empty jar means you are both more joyful, and that is good news for you.

Why? Well, let's say you have kept his joy level high, and he is coasting by on a cloud of love and appreciation. One day, you let him know while on your way to work that you want to head out for a drink with your girlfriends that evening. In this joyful state, he is all about making you happy, too, so he responds, "Have a great time." The joy has been multiplied.

Alternatively, let's say you are never home, you never help out, and you continue to do all the things that are filling up the Joy Jar. Then, you ask about that drink out. His response is not exactly full of joy: "Sure, go. Leave me here to handle everything. Have a great time."

Obviously, this is extreme marital sarcasm. He *doesn't* want you to have a good time. He may barely care if you make it back.

No joy = not good for you or your marriage.

When joy levels were low, it was clear to my spouse. He could read my vibe. He knew things were bad when he would be heading out for the day. He would look at my expression knowing I wasn't going to say anything and he would suggest, "So, don't die today," as we said goodbye. I would just nod. He had not respected me or my monkeys on that day and it had messed with my joy. My advice? Avoid this scenario.

For more information, turn to the Resource page.

If you haven't been to "The Monkeys: Building Intimacy and Trust" yet, please read now. Let's learn about a phrase you can use to save your sanity. Head to page 45 now.

INTIMACY

Intimacy. This is such a loaded word in relationships. It means something different to each person.

An oversimplified definition of it would be close familiarity, or friendship, or closeness. But in a marriage, it means a million little moments, touches, caresses, snuggles, and memories and neglects.

How can we foster closeness in the marriage? And how do we get them to recognize how important it is?

If your spouse doesn't enjoy touching (it's just not their jam), they can still choose to do it for you. It's when they know it is important to us and choose to ignore this need (or our begging and pleading) that we become desperate. They don't seem to realize the tenuous situation they are in, and all the while, we're getting close to the tipping point. The situation is becoming very black and white in our eyes.

Your options are:

1. Live like this for the rest of your life, never having authentic intimacy (add this your worksheet), or
2. Don't.

What do you choose? Go to Page 1, "Choose What Feels Right."

LOST WITH NO DIRECTION

So, you couldn't help yourself: you told them again, didn't you?

I know change is hard, but your need to be right does not enhance your intimacy and connection. The more you choose intimacy over being right, the closer you will become as a couple. In this example, you will both feel respected and loved.

The more you "help" them, the more you'll feel like their mother. And you don't want that—Intimacy Killer 101. That feeling of being desired and cherished starts with you. So, look in the mirror and try again.

Go back to Page 7, "Breaking Old Patterns" and choose the answer that leads to greater intimacy.

PRESENTS AND GIFTS AND TOKENS, OH MY!

If your love language is gifts, then you are making life very easy for your spouse: they just need to surprise you with a token of their love, and you are all set. Right?

The confusion comes in when we factor in frequency and value. This is where it is very important that you give details of what this act means to you. Add this detail to your worksheet and jot down some ways in which they can fulfill this love for you. It will help if they know how often and what kinds of gifts will do.

Also mention he can add reminders to his phone, so *he* gets reminded, but you still get the surprise. Maybe you only need a very thoughtful and expensive gift on the important dates, such as anniversaries, Valentine's, your birthday, and Christmas. Tell him that. Create an Amazon Wish List just for him. Maybe you like silly Post-it notes on your window, flowers for no reason, your favorite candy bar in your lunch, or him swinging by and bringing you coffee. If so, tell him this.

"Gifts" is a very broad category, and it is important that he understands what works for you. He could spend a lot of time choosing the wrong option and therefore feel like he is trying, while you're sitting around feeling like he doesn't care. Set the guidelines and be patient.

Include these guidelines in your conversation and add details or nudges in the Love Nudge app. Once it becomes second nature, you will be excited to see what's next, and he will enjoy thinking of things to give you.

Go to Page 29, "The Joy Jar" to add more joy.

IF YOU HAVE TO ASK...

Are a few moments, a few days, maybe a month, of good times in a year enough? Can this carry your marriage?

Answer this: Why are you still married? Did you get married to fight, argue, and be unhappy? Why have you stayed?

- He's a good provider, partner, and parent (if applicable). See Page 55, "Is This What I Signed Up For?"

- I can't do that to the kids. Divorce would be unfair to them. Go to Page 3, "The Time Has Come."

- No one is happy all the time. This is normal, even if I don't like it. Page 27, "Increasing Joy" is what you need.

PHYSICAL TOUCH

So, you aren't reading this book so you can leave things as they are. You want positive change and momentum. Physical Touch goes on your worksheet. It is a crucial topic.

Authentic physical touch goes both ways.

It may be that:

- You haven't mentioned that you are suffering silently. Now they will know, and together, you can work on a solution. It can be done.
- You've told them it matters many times, but nothing has changed. They did nothing differently and hoped you would just forget about it.

You have done what you needed to do. You've clearly stated your physical contact needs. That is all you can do. They'll either agree to adapt and use touch in a way that brings you closer, or they won't. The choice is in their hands. At the very least, they cannot claim they didn't know it was important.

I have another simple relationship tip on Page 29, "The Joy Jar."

Every woman deserves to be kissed, like it's the first time, and the last time, every time.

~Vesta

THE BENEFITS OF A FOOT-POPPING KISS

Well, at least you know you're a romantic. Not hopeless, I'd say, but hopeful. If you haven't expressed your definition in quite this way before, now is the time.

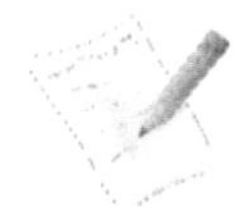

Kissing—real, romantic kissing—takes but a moment, but the effects are remarkable. One great, honest, loving kiss can leave me floating for days. It refills the love bank and makes me feel generous in return. It's a small price to pay on his part, and it reaps huge rewards.

What can he do to make you feel beautiful? Sexy? Wanted? Cherished? Chosen? All the above? Let him know. Fill out the worksheet.

Check out a few other intimacy builders on Page 29, "The Joy Jar."

THE MONKEYS: BUILDING INTIMACY AND TRUST

One way to build intimacy is through *trust*. When you question your spouse's motives, habits, and choices, they feel you do not trust them. How do you nip this in the bud? Well, sometimes, something comes up that is just *not* your problem. Really. It is *not yours*. I have a phrase to remind me to exercise trust instead of judgment.

Not my circus, not my monkeys.

Say it out loud. Repeat it. Let it sink in. Seems silly, right? But this is a marriage lifesaver. Saying this instead of whatever you want to say (trust me, he does *not* want to hear whatever "advice" you were going to give) does two things:

1. It stops any argument cold in its tracks. Suddenly, there is nothing to argue about.

2. It shows your spouse that you trust his decisions (even if deep down inside, you think you are *right* and he is wrong).

Maybe your spouse is about to make a smoothie. They've overfilled the container, *in your opinion*, and because you are always *right* and want to *help*, you are about to open your mouth to tell them that they are screwing up and are going to make a big mess.

But wait: you remember that being over-judgmental isn't going to help.

Instead, do nothing, look away if you have to, and do *not* give your *advice*.

Meanwhile, your spouse knows your "I told you so" is pending and is waiting for you to offer your "advice." They are prepared for you to throw the first "know it all" verbal punch. There is tension in the air. What they don't know is that you have already remembered your new mantra: *Not my circus, not my monkeys.* This is their circus. You are just in the audience. Smile and go about your business. Nothing to see here, folks. It will be hard, but the good news is it will get easier, and it will bring more joy to you both.

Now, here's the hard part: if or when the smoothie overflows and makes a mess, *do not*:

1. Say "I told you so" or "I was going to tell you."
2. Laugh and point.
3. ...Or anything else!

It is not your circus or they are not your monkeys. If your spouse makes a mess, they will clean it up, and anything you say will start a fight. Practice not giving your opinion in these situations. This way, you will slowly rebuild that trust from all the times you *didn't* keep quiet.

If you have not yet read Page 25, "Create Your New Future," do so now. If you have, turn to Page 7, "Breaking Old Patterns"

ARE YOU IN OR OUT?

PAINT THAT ROOM!

If you feel loved when your spouse does things for you, then you are in luck. Generally speaking, most men like showing love in tangible ways. It is very easy to feel loved if your spouse already knows how to do the thing that will make you feel loved. If you need them to build a shelf, they'll say, "Where is my saw?" If you need them to paint the bathroom, they'll say, "What color?" They can quickly grasp that this act will lead to you feeling loved. They also get that when you feel loved, you are more likely to love them back, in *their* best way.

If this is your love language, then be clear about how you feel loved, and ask how they would like you to share it with them. The Love Nudge app, for example, is an easy way to communicate; or maybe they just need a simple to-do list.

Add this to your worksheet and discuss it. I think most husbands will find this clarity a godsend and will jump at the chance to make you happy.

If they don't love it but are willing to try, be patient and start small.

Go to Page 29, "The Joy Jar" to add more joy daily.

Money does not define a relationship, but shared values around it determine whether two people can build a future.

~ Elle Lundy

FUNDING YOUR FUTURE

The best way to talk about money is to decide what your common goals are. You could start with some resources on the Resource page. You could also seek an advisor or make an appointment with your current advisor.

If only one person has been "in charge," you might discuss how to allocate or share responsibilities. If no one is the boss and no one is on an allowance, working toward shared goals becomes a great motivator. Agreeing on how you want to spend, save, and invest your hard-earned salaries will bring a lot of peace. It will become the bedrock of your renewed relationship.

Check out Page 29, "The Joy Jar" for more joyful tips.

I used to love you to the very top of my heart but slowly I lowered my standards as disappointment arrived. Breaking the pattern means choosing differently not loving less.

~ Elle Lundy

LEVEL OF JOY

What can you do to break patterns? Shake things up! Check out "The Joy Jar" and "The Monkeys: Building Intimacy and Trust." The little things help keep more love in and make each day a little better.

I used to tell my husband when we woke up, "I love you to the very top, up to one hundred percent. Then twenty percent less when I trip over his shoes by the door, and then ten percent less when I must unfold his dirty socks to wash them. I also love him a little less when I must clean up his smoothie blender, and so on, until he comes home and doesn't know why he is getting the cold shoulder. "

A better way of expressing your needs is using the Joy Jar and the idea of the monkeys. These allow you to take back your life and love and to build a stronger, more intimate relationship. Visit page 29 and 45.

Love is giving someone all the power over you to destroy you and praying they won't hurt you.

~Reagan Michelle Lundy

IS THIS WHAT I SIGNED UP FOR?

I am sure he's a good guy. You picked him to share your life with, after all. You knew what you were doing when you made that decision. He sometimes (or all the time) helps around the house, with the kids (if applicable), with the pets, and with laundry. He isn't doing anything wrong; you just feel you're not connected. But what does "connected" mean to you?

- It means intimacy. All of it: touching, caresses, closeness, talking of our future, talking about everything and nothing, and sharing and trusting. Go to Page 33, "Intimacy."

- It means touch. All of it: lovemaking, sex, holding hands (by choice!), and a general feeling of being chosen every day and cherished. Go to Page 15, "As Olivia Sang, "Let's Get Physical!"

- It means him kissing me goodbye like it might be our last, and him kissing me like he's been gone a year and never wants to let go again when he comes home. Go to Page 43, "The Benefits of a Foot-Popping Kiss."

- It means more quality time with him. Go to Page 9, "Quality Time"
- It means him doing things for me. Go to Page 49, "Paint That Room!"
- It means him getting me presents, or thoughtful little gifts. Go to Page 37, "Presents and Gifts and Tokens, Oh My!"
- If you find your joy slips throughout the day because of his behaviors. Go to Page 53, " Level of Joy"

MOVING ON

Well, I did ask you to be honest. If this is how you feel, let's save everyone some time and get right to it.

You have let your partner know you do not want to stay married. You have decided that you want an amicable, fair, drama-free divorce. That is the only respectful choice.

You are grateful for:

- The time you've had together.
- The life you've shared.
- The family you've created (if applicable).

Seek mediation to finalize your divorce. Do not be petty or vengeful here. Be fair. Be quick. Remind yourself why you loved them and show respect when you speak about them and to them. Be the best version of yourself as you move on. Your kids are watching (if you have them), and they will remember how you both conduct yourselves during this time.

Ladies, if you reach this page and you know it is the right path for you, I want you to have the most powerful information before you begin. I offer a soothing and supportive environment to assist you during these next steps and to protect you in the process. To schedule a private call with Vesta head to www.vestatalks.com.

Life is too wide and beautiful to spend it in a love
that feels small.

~Elle Lundy

RESOURCE PAGE

Couples' Books

- The 5 Love Languages: The Secret to Love that Lasts by Gary Chapman (1990, Northfield Publishing)

- Smart Couples Finish Rich: 9 Steps to Creating a Rich Future for You and Your Partner by David Bach (2001, Broadway)

- Start Late, Finish Rich: A No-Fail Plan for Achieving Financial Freedom at Any Age by David Bach (2005, Doubleday Canada)

- The Finish Rich Workbook: Get Out of Debt, Put Your Dreams in Action and Achieve Financial Freedom by David Bach (2005, Doubleday Canada)

Ladies' Books

- Lucky Bitch: A Guide for Exceptional Women to Create Outrageous Success by Denise Duffield-Thomas (2011, Kindle Edition)

*Note: I am not affiliated with, nor do I receive sponsorship from, any of these resources.

- Get Rich, Lucky Bitch: Release Your Money Blocks and Live a First-Class Life by Denise Duffield-Thomas (2013, Kindle Edition)

- Excuse Me, Your Life Is Waiting: The Astonishing Power of Feelings by Lynn Grabhorn (1999, Beyond Books)

- You Are a Badass: How to Stop Doubting Your Greatness and Start Living an Awesome Life by Jen Sincero (2013, Running Press Adult)[2]

- Give Yourself a Raise: The Mindset and Math You Need to Get to Your First Million by Erin B. Haag (2023, Pricing Overhaul, LLC)

- Unleashed: Tapping into your feminine instinct to create financial independence by Yulin Lee (2022, Beyond Publishing)

Apps

Love Nudge is connected to Chapman's *The 5 Love Languages*. Take the quiz and share your love language with your spouse. Stay connected to your spouse and show love the way *they* feel it. Set goals and nudge each other to build your healthy relationship.

*All of Jen Sincero's books kick you in the butt, and her merchandise is super-fun!

Retreats and Adventures

The W.I.N. Marriage Adventure was created by Vesta Rachael Gauntlett.

This is more than a marriage retreat. It is an exclusive event featuring marriage workshops, unique experiences, and crafting a plan for your future.

These retreats are held throughout the year, and their limited availability allows for dedicated couples to enjoy this experience, grow, and reconnect. See website for details, and to reserve your spot. www.vestatalks.com/events.

Podcasts

You can also explore the But First...Champagne podcast. This is hosted by me and is a space where we celebrate women who are living their best life and where we no longer accept the minimization of our successes.

In these episodes, I interview amazing women, to inspire every woman listening to reach for her dreams. If you are one of these women or know someone to recommend, please reach out to me. www.vestatalks.com

I've played all my cards and that's what you've done too. Nothing more to say, no more ace to play.

~ As sung by ABBA

ABOUT THE AUTHOR

Vesta Gauntlett is an author, speaker, and retreat host who helps couples courageously ask the question many avoid: Are we In or Out?

She is the creator of the W.I.N. Marriage Adventure (What Is Next), an intimate luxury experience designed to help couples reconnect, rediscover their spark, and intentionally design an exciting future together.

Through her work, Vesta encourages couples to choose their relationship with clarity, courage, and a little adventure.

Vesta splits her time between the Pacific and Inland Northwest with her family and is looking forward to her next adventure.